AF375210

NATURE'S VOICES

NATURE'S VOICES

Illustrated Poems Inspired by the Natural World

MEGAN DESROSIERS

HERBAL BONES ART

Herbal Bones Art, LLC
herbalbonesart.com

Copyediting by Aaron Lelito
Illustrations by Megan Desrosiers

A CIP record for this book is available from the Library of Congress Cataloging-in-Publication Data

ISBN-13: 979-8-9929909-3-5

for my grandmother

these words are not my own,
they are gifts from Nature
received during the interstitial
and quiet moments
that are possible
when we slow down

Contents

Ready for Flight

Wise Giants

Mullein: A Love Affair

Preface

You may think that *Gardens of the Underworld* was written before *Nature's Voices*, but in truth, it was the other way around. Many of these poems were written before or during the early stages of writing *Gardens of the Underworld* but, as I lovingly say, the poisonous plants bullied me into completing their collection first. It does not mean that the messages shared herein are not as important but rather that the poisonous plants were more urgent in their sharing.

I mentioned in the preface to *Gardens of the Underworld* that I had not considered myself a poet when the plants first approached me to collaborate and share their words and voices. "Dance of the Maple Seed" was written first. I could see an elegant woman slowly twirling down toward earth, as her ballroom skirts billowed around her. It was such a beautiful image, but it was something I initially chose not to share. I was still new to this way of receiving and sharing, and I was not sure of my voice or of how it would be received.

As I sat outside early one morning a couple of weeks later, Mullein offered me the second poem: "I am Mullein." Sunlight was refracting through the prisms of the raindrops scattered across Mullein's giant fuzzy leaves and creating tiny rainbows. Still uncertain, I shared this poem with my friend, Ravina, who provided me with some much-needed encouragement. I suppose my soul responded on some level with a "yes" because shortly thereafter I found myself in a strange love affair with a single Mullein that I regularly passed on my neighborhood walks.

The number of Mullein poems and the others grow over the subsequent months. I moved them around quite a bit, uncertain as to what the final collection would look like or if the early poems belonged to an entirely different collection. Once *Gardens of the Underworld* was complete, however, I was able to see with clarity not only which poems belonged where but also that I had somehow completed not just one but three additional volumes of poetry.

I think we are sometimes in denial of who we are because it either comes easily, or we have a fear of being seen for who we are. My natal moon is in Pisces in the ninth house. This has been reflected to me as being someone who is "poetic to no end." When I first read that meaning, it didn't make sense to me. Now, even if I still harbor some doubts, I do understand just how much my soul wants to poetically express the inspiration of the world around us.

A moment toward the end of the editing process stands out in my mind. I am seated at the kitchen table, laptop and coffee near at hand. Instead of feeling the bliss and fulfillment of the moment at having completed my edits, I was stuck in looping thoughts of self-doubt. I couldn't understand how and why I had been chosen to share these voices, something so incredibly sacred. I sensed movement out the window and looked up. Flying by in their massive and graceful beauty was the brilliant black and red of a pileated woodpecker. I can regularly find them in the trees when I follow the source of their loud calls; however, it is somewhat rare for me to see one fly across my path. The message was clear: the collection was complete.

Thank you for being curious about what the green beings, winged ones, and creepy crawly ones have to say, and for reading my own collaborative interpretations of their words. May these words speak to you and inspire you to begin your own observational listening and walking practice among the sentient beings who reside in the natural world.

One Divinity

Plants don't have mouths,
let us offer ours.
Animals have sound
but no distinct language.
Let them use our voices—
let us share their words,
not interpretations.

Let them speak through us
as vessels and channels.
Let them guide us
in healing and rejoicing.
For when we rejoice together,
we sing and dance together—
a language understood by all.

No words necessary,
a common threshold—
you can cross if you believe
in them and in their voices.
Believe in their community—
in their community as our community,
in Our community as One.

Fairies Be Here

Fairies are commonly found
in the woods, wilder places,
and near plants with which
they have special affinities.

If you are true of heart,
have patience and luck, then
one day you may have the honor
of making their acquaintance.

Hosta House

It's raining, join us
under the great big leaves
greens and whites, blues too
pretty umbrellas just for you.

It's sunny, come
under the shade enjoy
the bees and butterflies
stay cool, safe from prying
eyes hungry, diving birds.

It's windy, hold on
don't blow away
the tall stalks stand firm
as air swirls round, laugh
out loud in giddy joy.

Tinkling rain
simmering sun
fierce wind—
no matter the weather
we do it all from here.

Queen Anne's Arrival

an eye watches and waits
anticipates the moment
of arrival
the time to curtsy, bow
and nod—to open
just for you

Elecampane Portal

Just your height—
we came down for you,
just for you to sip sunshine
and slip through.

Enter the portal
into a world of delight
meant for you,
we came down for you.

Queen Anne's Lace

Bullseye, the center
pulls and sucks you in.
The path is clear but use care,
don't resist the fall.

I'll swallow you whole
with a lick, a gulp
and a slurp.

Softer edges than you think,
constriction tighter
tighter.

Go in this side
then out the other
in one single burst.

Queen Anne's Chariot

Constellations of starlight
are a bright wand
just for you.

Bend down and pluck it
when no one looks
and grasp me tight—
it's time to start
your journey.

No need to hurry
but don't be late.
Your white scepter,
chariot and flight
to our world await.

Beltane Hawthorn

Celebrate in the flowers
hold your wand high.
Come, join us—
twirl in the twilight
dance until dawn.
We're waiting for you.

Lady's Slippers

step out in your dainty
slippers reach for the
stars twirl and
dance with us

Wildflower Meadows

smile and play
in delightful sunshine
sway to the rhythms
the everlasting breath
the heartbeat of
the earth

Dance of the Wild Rose

Swing in the breeze
and sunshine—
that yellow delight.
Dance your quiet jig
bent knees, kicked feet
breathe deep
sing joyful with us.

Hawthorn Flower Dance

Dance!
Dance in a circle,
rose wand held high!
So high!

Dance!
'til we fall and die—
Death is a portal,
a beginning, a newness
and an oldness at once.

So dance! Dance!
Dance in a circle
with us!

Queen Bee Balm

Towering over me like a Queen
'til the groundnut took her down,
tumbling her crown

her beauty swaying in the wind,
swaying
swaying
all the way down

down

down

to the ground.

Echinacea Bee Dreams

Poor dear
working so hard she fell asleep
among the flower tops.
Shhhh—don't startle her,
she's dreaming her beautiful dreams.
Let her doze and slowly wake
stretching and lingering,
in sweet nighttime memories.

Ancient Ones

these creepy and crawly ancients
hold the wisdom of the earth
each is worthy of more
than a moment of your time

Restful Bee

this backward bend
is a fine view of what's below
savor this time, pause and dangle—
kiss the wind as the moon and stars
all wait to say
hello

House Spider

twilight is the time to feast
to drink deep of memories
as they twist, struggle and
resist death's call, quietly
I soothe them to sleep

Garden Spider

Neon green and yellow flash
across soft hues of dawn.

Patiently swaying atop
silk threads of silver dew.

The heart beats in cycles
in this dance with death.

Stinkbug

Hardened
on your back on the floor
arms and legs rigid
frailly clinging inward.
Should I have set you free?
Would you have frozen out there
or were you hungry, trapped inside—
slowly starved for more?

Spiderweb at Dawn

pearls weave across time
dewdrops sigh in the morning sun
words whispered out of the past
prophecies declared about a future
linger and doze in crystalline dreams
with tales to spin, wisdom to share
between the seconds of your life
as they tick-tick-tick away

Gray Treefrog

Deep wells of memory
stare out from the lichen,
eyes that carry the sorrow
and grief we each bear.

Their voices trill brightly
piercing the consuming dark;
they sing of promised hope
and of life yet to breathe.

Share in joyful song,
forget your despair—
join their splendid chorus
on this sovereign night.

Turtle Eggs

intentional
brick by brick
stone by solid stone
strong foundations
birth organic creations
as nature transforms
the impermanence of time

Black Snake

Thickly twining up my feet, calves and legs
the trance cools around my bareness,
a lullaby of dark memories stirred
from beneath—spin among the stars
to remember and release.
Learn to shed and show
your tender bright skin.

Ground Beetle

You lay there, legs kicking
struggling at the curb
uncertain of your fate.

I ponder the next refrain—
the expected coda and
decide to intervene.

A gentle flip and you persist
in your slow trek across
a hard, black expanse.

Black Ants

one by two by three by four and evermore
left right, left right, march across the floor
there's food ahead, the mission today

let's make the climb up the wall—
claim the prize our queen demands

we swarm, left right, left right
on and on through the night
hurry now, stay in line
work together, carry your weight

our strength will see this through

left right, left right
on and on each day and night

Skill of the Garter Snake

Intensity and focus, persevere
to catch the prize you must wait,
gauge the striking moment.

Too soon, too late
and it's all in vain.

Stay low to find balance,
the finish and perfection are
a finesse between the two.

Horsefly

with agile speed
adapt and grow
dart and dive
toward your goal
dare to believe
persist tenaciously
it's yours if you could
only see

Ready for Flight

moving above and between worlds
our feathered friends return
with messages from the beyond

The Authenticity of the Crow

Slow down
speak authentic truth
prepare for hard work
devotion and lifelong pursuit.
It can be yours and will be magic.
I'm waiting, the world awaits.
Are you ready?
Let's go!

The Crow Dare

Strutting back and forth,
parading, waiting, teasing
sipping the water
playfully
testing with my toes.

I'm pretty and I know it.
Look at me.
I'm handsome—
you know it.

I'm all in, expect you
to follow me into the puddle.
The water's just fine—
don't you know?

Blue Heron Oracle

The mystery lies within
the liminal and physical.
Move in-between
slip back out—
now you see me
now you don't.
To access your depths
simply close your eyes—
disappear.

Crow Flight

follow me into the void
ride into expectant darkness
shimmer and glamour await

it's time
fly with me
glide down low
among flowers
and high above trees
swoop through clouds
then come back to me
take this witch's trip
and you will learn
all that's in you

time to see

Blue Heron Discernment

Only in great calmness
can you see the wider frame.
Stay still to choose
move slowly, carefully.
The path calls at the tip
of your toe. You are ready,
turn your head just so.
Step forward unwary
with deliberate
knowing.

Wild Turkeys

bob and weave, dart through
with eyes wide, we freeze
not a breath—they'll see

paused, neck craning
seeking who's there

run forward again
the chasing wind
pushes us to the trees

The Huntress

silently watching
head slowly turning
large golden eyes pierce
where no one else can see

patiently waiting
acutely listening—
tiny feet in dry leaves
feel safe, they don't know
I'm here

a subtle shift of air
a stab of soft warmth
then gently lifting back
to my tree

Vultures

Silently soaring and watching,
protecting and honoring
your wisdom and belief,
grasp of the cycle.

Rising higher and higher,
we feed the circle of life
and death—
connecting all.

Twin Cormorants

wings outstretched
                    atop your perches
   beaks held high
              seeking the sun

    basking in pouring rain
    feathers ruffle in
                        wind
                  mist
                  cleansing
                      waters

    air and dry what you can
    it's time:
            dive
               again

Wren Song

When the rains have passed
yet still linger in your mind,
a small bird bubbles with song
memories that smile under a
glorious sun.

They scold you: *open the curtains,*
dry your tears, the gloom is gone.
The little wren sings
of days to come.

Pileated Woodpecker

cuk cuks, wuk wuks, and piping calls
urge from the wild edge:
cast your inside voice away
it's time to laugh and play
spread your wings
release your fears
run for joy
whoop loud and clear
merrily join us
under the tall trees

Robin Egg

look at you:
small and blue
just birthed into
our world potential
is ahead little bird—
flying high, where
will you go?

Hawk

the true goal, the path ahead
is unseen yet felt and known
discernment brings you
to the sun over the next ridge
use your gifts, focus your eyes
it's time to glide home

Gifts

Floating from the sky
resting on the pavement
hanging from a blade of grass
drifting against stiff leaves—
solitary feathers are daily
reminders of the guided
steady path that leads
closer to home.

Wise Giants

moving much slower than others
in decades of quiet observation
with a watchful eye and broad perspective
trees have an unsurpassed, ancient wisdom

The Three-Toed Leaves of Sassafras

Dinosaurs still roam the earth
not as birds, as trees—
three-toed trees with three-toed leaves
move quietly through the night.
Three-toed trees with three-toed leaves
move quietly each and every night.

Winter Trees

Gnarled and twisted hands,
arms painfully reaching
to the sky—
they seek the healing,
the warmth and blessings
that the sun brings.

"Gaia holds too much
pain," the trees
whisper, desiring
to flee the prison
of our fate.

Blueberry

We're different yet held
together on a single stem:
big
small
colorful
plump
tight

no matter
the shape, the color
we all belong.

Diving Trees

They say trees reach to the sky
but I see trees that descend into earth
a reflection of humanity's need
to dive
deep
down
into the ground
to compost our old ways
so we can emerge into
our coming spring.

Tulip Poplar Wands

Sword play and magic wands
these portals to the Otherworld
are fragile and easily missed,
even scattered at your feet.

Remember the path
is at your tippy toes—
move your feet and your head
but keep your eyes closed.

Trust yourself, step
forward in the dark
slowly inch onward
using full intention.

Rest with Me

Forget the ants
tickling our feet,
making us laugh—
be still, stand
like me high above
the other trees.

In order to see
you must slow down—
come breathe
inhale, exhale
you and I as one,
release, rest with me.

Autumn Oak Leaf

        suspended
     gliding
sighing

  as everyone skitters

      below

  I am

    suspended

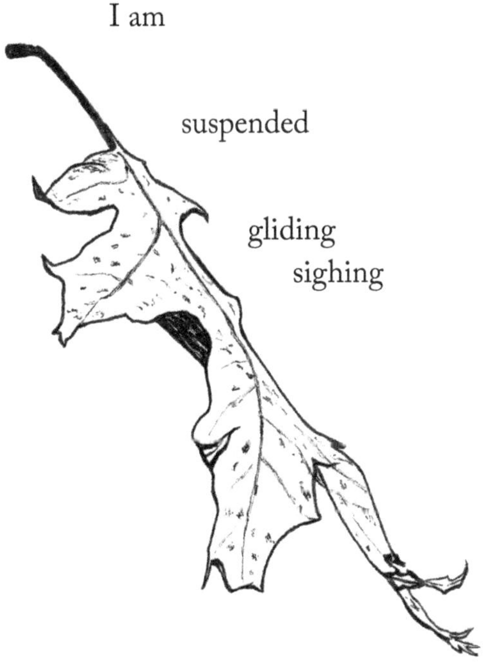

     gliding
      sighing

Dance of the Maple Seed

Time is standing still
I'm slowly spinning
gracefully twirling
delicately dancing—
where I land
I do not know.

Sunlit Canopy

stand under us
we will bathe and shower you
in loving light you're deserving
of radiance it's brilliant
in this divine embrace

Linden

I looked up
and there you were,
have always been
supporting me.

Weeping Willow

long arms droop, drape
around, caressing skin, hair
intertwined in swaying leaves
cascading tears, rivers collecting
at your roots, mingling deep
in black earth, the damp soil
shifts as I stand and lean
once more walking toward
a freedom found in the
dawning morn

Pine Sap

step inside the resinous drop
enter the tiny house, clear your mind
dissolve your sorrows and worries
down the deep, thick root
refresh your mind, receive
immortal wisdom from above
brighter days will soon shine on you

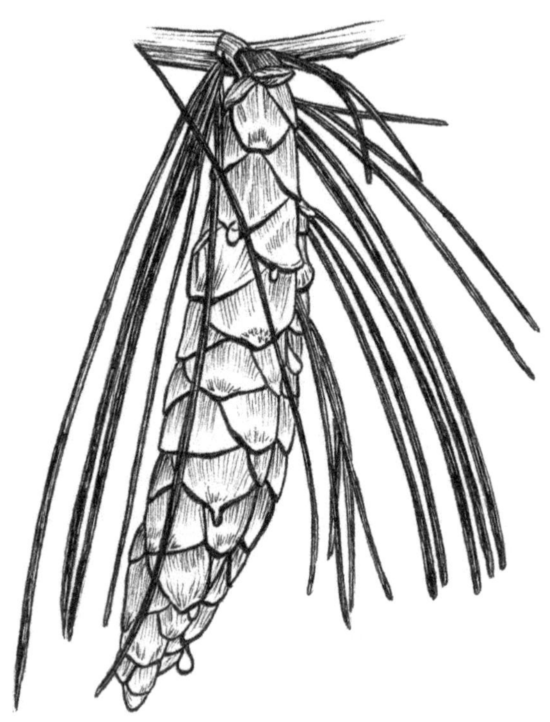

Oak Gall

This ink of truth is no facsimile
it's your own innate wisdom
use it with patience and care.

Paper may thin, crumble and tear.
Oh, but that creative moment
of moving pigment across the page!

You find your voice when connected
with earth wisdom and the words come
from deep within.

Sun Halo

golden, glowing
emanating from within
we are starlight, not stardust
our hearts light the way,
we are reflections of the heavens
and celestial reminders of
Divinity

Mullein: A Love Affair

the words herein
document the strange love
affair between a human
and a mullein plant

I Am Mullein

I am Mullein with thousands
of diamonds in my hair
rising softly gently
                softly gently—

honoring the Queen
the Mother in all I am
Mullein.

Morning Light

reaching toward the light
with delight shaking it off
stretching arms wide awake
then lulled back to sleep

Crisis

Who am I?
You are you, I am I
names are irrelevant.

You're unique
stand tall proud
out in the crowd.

The Realization

Walking by almost every day
you reach to me,
I to you branching
upward and outward toward me
yet remaining deeply rooted
unmoving bold and tall.

I desire your embrace
but keep going while longing
to remain in place with you
always I think I am falling
in love.

The Reflection

I started small full
of potential everyone starts
small wound tight waits
to spring forth in slow motion
a strong base you've got
the pieces big leaves touch
light you are the light.

I love you too.

Gossip

Don't touch me getting
taller I remain boundaried
in stillness not retreating
or hiding,
rise above the chatter
the pulling and prying,
rise above it all.

Despair

my Husband, "the town
mowed today," I didn't
piece it together the knot
growing as I rounded
the corner you were gone
taken without goodbye,
our love affair over

I'll visit you
in our dreams

Doppleganger

under this warm snug rock
I could rest linger forever
full of love true love
more than roses or violets
grounded in your embrace
I'm yours alone yours,
the one you miss is me,
stay keep me warm
a while longer

Lingering

I'm still here you're still
here it makes me happy
lingering together before
it's over not to worry
I'll be here different
but waiting for you
always

Faith

They keep cutting me down,
don't understand like you wounded
over and over with scars
each tenacious return with strength
resilience and learning
how to build and renew
faith in self, in each other
in what we have to do.

The Return

Death: a temporary subtle energetic
shift the trauma and pain make us
stronger those scars and wounds
that no one else can see
are meant to be
you and me.

We come back more
beautiful and splendid than before
with stories and adventures
to share no fuss
understand the journey death
transforms each day.

Bloom

Don't lose faith
nothing lives forever
we can return rebirth
grow climb high tall
bloom again,

be seen for who
you are soft beauty
reaching great heights
strengthen as you soften
bloom once more.

Belief

True wealth is intricate
tiny diamonds reflecting
inherent beauty your love
for all beings, community,
gaze into these jewels
fill up believe in these
reflections of you.

Acknowledgements

I am in deep gratitude to the spirits of the land on which I reside. I am merely passing through the place you have resided for hundreds, if not thousands of years. I am humbled that you have chosen to share your voices with me with the request that I share them with others. It has been and continues to be an honor to continue to collaborate with you.

I don't even know how to begin to thank the helping spirits, guides, and wise and well ancestors who continue to guide me in this incarnation. I don't quite know where we are headed but I know your guidance is keeping me aligned with the path forward with each step we take together.

Thank you, dear reader, for choosing to pick up this book and see the world through a different lens. Thank you for your continued support of these creative collaborations with the non-human realms. I am blessed to know that others are curious to learn how to communicate with the plant and animal spirits. May this collaboration help you to believe that it is possible and that you aren't making it up. Imagination became the "safe" way to connect for far too long. Know that your imagination is more alive than you've been led to believe.

Thank you, dear Ravina. I had so much fear around sharing my voice when I first began writing poetry. You provided the perfect amount of sacred witnessing and encouragement when I shared those first few poems with